Unconventional Wisdom

To: Muriel

— With best wishes.

Glenn Ferguson

16 OCT 99

Unconventional Wisdom

A Primer of Provocative Aphorisms

Glenn Ferguson

A PenArtPro Book
Pen Art Productions, Inc.
Tempe, Arizona
www.penartpro.com

© 1999 by Glenn Ferguson
Second Printing

All rights exclusively reserved. No part of this book may be reproduced or translated into any language or utilized in any form or by any means, electronic or mechanical, including photocopying, recording or by any information storage and retrieval system, without permission in writing from the publisher.

A PenArtPro Book
Published by Pen Art Productions, Inc.
Tempe, Arizona
www.penartpro.com

Library of Congress Cataloging-in-Publication Data

Unconventional wisdom: a primer of provocative aphorisms/ by Glenn Ferguson

ISBN 1-893302-02-4

1. Aphorisms 2. Philosophy

LC Number 99-070276
Unconventional Wisdom by Glenn Ferguson

Cover and Book Design by The Roberts Group
Printed by Lightning Print, Inc.
Printed in the United States of America

An aphorism is a flight of wit and so is life.

Preface

FOR TWENTY YEARS, I HAVE PREPARED A DAILY JOURNAL ENTRY. In a few cases I have captured the personal events of the day. More frequently, I have resorted to topical essays involving a diversity of subjects. Whenever I happen to turn a phrase that captures my attention, I note "aphorism" as part of the indexing process. This volume incorporates the aphorisms which I believe represent my style and prejudices.

Unless the author has obtained notoriety through media coverage, the compiler of aphorisms is placed at a serious disadvantage. If you are unknown, what you write is of little interest to the typical reader. If you write it with a twist, it still produces a collective yawn from the reading public.

Writers of aphorisms, restricted to limited reputations, have resorted to subterfuge to peddle their wares. In recent years, you may have noticed little volumes bearing "maxims, proverbs, witticisms, analects, sayings, epigrams, axioms, bon

PREFACE

mots, adages or apothegms" in the title. Without the odor of fame, aphorisms by any other name are still aphorisms.

In the absence of a substantial market, I have attempted to confuse the potential reader by alleging that the wisdom contained herein is "unconventional" or possibly "provocative." Whichever evasion of the truth induced you to come along for the ride, I am hopeful that you will agree that Americans need to make fun of themselves. Life is too important to approach it without a semblance of wit.

Glenn Ferguson

Table of Contents

Preface	7
AGE	**13**
Youth	14
Maturity	16
Senility	17
NOW AND THEN	**21**
Life	22
Death	24
Religion	25
FRIENDS AND REPUTATION	**27**
SOCIETY	**29**
Receptions	31
Fashion	32
Happiness	33
Matrimony	34
Waste	35
Noise	36

TABLE OF CONTENTS

Violence	37
Loneliness	38
Humor	39

HOUSE AND HOME — 41

LEISURE TIME — 43

Art	44
Food	45
Sports	46
Holidays and Travel	47

HEALTH — 49

THE THREE R'S ET AL — 51

Thinking	52
Reading	54
Writing	55
Speaking	57
Words	59
The Media	62

DREAMS — 65

TABLE OF CONTENTS

BELIEFS	67
VIRTUE	69
VICE	71
THE DISCIPLINES	73
History	74
Education	76
DISCRIMINATION	79
Blacks	81
Women	82
WORK AND COMPENSATION	83
The Work Ethic	84
Organization and Management	86
Business	88
Money	90
CHARITY	93

TABLE OF CONTENTS

THE PUBLIC WEAL   95
Democracy   96
Government   98
Politics   99

THE WORLD OUTSIDE   101
Foreign Relations   102
International Affairs   104
The Developing World   105

ABOUT THE AUTHOR   107

Age

AGE/YOUTH

Youth

If I were a child again, I would remain in third grade.

Teenagers can rise to the occasion even when the occasion does not demand it.

Youth is only wasted on the young when the young fail to prepare for maturity.

If children are exposed to reasonable adults, they will grow up reasonably.

Youth represents violent frustration evolving from unrequited expectation.

AGE / YOUTH

Sun tanning is associated with youthful fantasies at any age.

A generous dose of youthful energy would postpone old age.

Until age intervenes, the new generation is hopeful.

AGE/MATURITY

Maturity

I have no idea what I want be when I grow up, but I missed the deadline.

I am too young to be growing old.

Maturity and survival are synonyms.

A sense of timing grows with maturity.

When I change my mind, that is maturity. When you change yours, that is duplicity.

As we age, we see our previous tracks, but we cannot retrace them.

Time frays memory of paternal concern.

AGE/SENILITY

Senility

Senility is a frame of mind rather than a function of age.

Some are senile at twenty. Others are "young" at the age of senility.

The selected memory of age is a blessing in disguise.

The secret of longevity is to throw out the junk mail unopened and to ignore television commercials.

As we age, we save things. When we are old, we dispose of them.

The secret of meaningful old age is to handle pain.

There is a direct correlation between age and the number of pills.

AGE / SENILITY

Adjustment to physical changes makes one feel old.

When illness intervenes, age precludes creativity.

Reading, writing and running — a prescription for survival.

Retirement is a figment of the imagination.

Retirement commitments expand to fill leisure.

My only fear of retirement is that I may not live to enjoy it.

When a person reaches retirement, never ask his age. You will hear more than you want to know.

Successful retirement requires well-honed avocational interests.

At retirement, trees rather than watches should be awarded.

Growing old does not lead to mellowness.

Age is considered an asset until it becomes a liability.

Growing old is a perception as well as a reality.

AGE / SENILITY

To be forgotten, rather than forgetting, is the curse of old age.

Survival, not retribution, is the only vindication.

The only way to get even is to outlive your enemies.

Now and Then

Life

Life should be a quest rather than a cop-out.

We lead lives of comfortable superficiality.

Life is optimistic self-restraint following unfulfilled dreams.

Seasonal variation illustrates the cyclical as well as the fleeting meaning of life.

Life is amazingly complicated and unusually bleak.

Life is a subliminal passing of years.

Memory does not sustain. Anticipation does not reassure. Life is now.

NOW AND THEN / LIFE

The six stages of life:

- Childhood—Tilting at potential with a lollipop.

- Adolescence—Making obscene gestures at precedence.

- Young adulthood—Extolling the sensual with intellectual arrogance.

- Maturity—Striving for the mundane in a cocoon of prejudice.

- Senior citizenry—Vegetating with earned superiority.

- Senility—Grasping for amorphous straws.

Death

Obituaries should be released when you retire, not when you expire.

Funerals should honor the living, not the dead.

Nothing is certain except death and taxes, and even taxes lack clarity.

We are remembered for the blatant rather than the important.

Species extinction is preferable to zoo preservation.

Death by accident is part of life. Death in war is a crime.

Religion

Religion imposes a subjective interpretation of the unknown.

When religion becomes conviction, acumen disappears.

Natural law is a codification of social norms.

Paradise allows for a great margin of error.

Heathens disbelieve popular fables and believe unpopular fables.

Restraint on sin results from societal pressure rather than religious credo.

What did God do prior to the first day?

Heaven and Hell reside in each of us, in variable doses.

Heaven expresses an unattainable dream. Hell represents a living reality.

Miracles are never justified rationally.

Although man has trod upon it, a full moon represents faith as well as fact.

The diversity of human faces is a true miracle.

Bible reading should require a prescription.

The Golden Rule represents good sense, not the will of God.

When dictionaries rather than bibles are placed in hotel rooms, civilization may survive.

When you feel discouraged, think of the men and women "of the cloth."

Sectarian charity is merely human courtesy.

A typical sermon incorporates the vocabulary of basic English.

In vitro is the closest approximation of a virgin birth, and yet some church groups oppose the process.

Friends and Reputation

If dogs were able to talk, they would cease to be man's best friends.

A friend calls you when he or she is unemployed. A good friend calls you when you are unemployed.

Friends in need provoke irrational arguments indeed.

To develop close friends, discuss everything except yourself.

A mimeographed message from alleged friends fails to capture the spirit of Christmas.

Respect requires distance from others.

The more significant the attainment, the fewer the friends.

FRIENDS AND REPUTATION

Because you believe it, praise is a blessing.

Reputation and reality are antonyms.

We believe the worst about those whom we do not know.

Prominence is the only benefit of prominence.

The only thing duller than meeting celebrities is reading about them.

Hubris outranks humility; therefore, celebrities create their own epitaphs.

Notoriety converts acquaintances to friends.

Society

Humanity is lovable. The individuals are suspect.

The aberrant is becoming the norm.

When the angels want to punish, they give us success or good looks.

Infinity: Waiting for a critical telephone call.

Is anybody really interested in the other guy?

I repudiate American society, but I am proud to be an American.

The slander of the covetous crowd is omnipresent.

A society that treats Madonna as a heroine deserves its plight.

Sham controls most social interaction.

SOCIETY

If I could protect my loved ones, pauperism would be attractive.

There are so few with power who care.

Receptions

At cocktail parties we ignore those whom we do not recognize.

Receptions attract people who want to impress others rather than those who are interested in others.

A successful reception requires servitude by the host and hostess.

SOCIETY/FASHION

Fashion

If you dress like the other guy, you may begin to sound like the other guy.

His heritage prepared him to be out of fashion, and he honed the gift to perfection.

Happiness

A sense of well-being beats sex.

Happiness is time and space.

It is discouraging how unhappy most humans appear to be.

Matrimony

When marriage works, a miracle occurs. There are few miracles.

Marriage involves relationship, not gender.

If you can listen without considering substance, matrimony can succeed.

Marriage is a way of life, not a sexual bond.

The modern family: an inter-racial lesbian married couple acquiring progeny by artificial insemination.

Waste

We live in a world half-depraved and half-debris.

Solid waste: one of mankind's most significant accomplishments.

The Earth is threatened by human waste more than human aggression.

Noise

Henry Thoreau did not cope with chain saws, gas mowers and earthmovers.

The definition of noise: two children in a swimming pool.

It is impossible to escape the omnipresence of machines.

Violence

Violence draws unthinking humans like flies.

Human beings will engage in inhuman behavior until external power intervenes.

If we perfected inter-personal relationships the way we perfect wine, aggression would disappear.

Casual killing is no worse than casual conception.

Never ask a person pointing a gun to explain the indiscretion.

Loneliness

The ultimate loneliness is being part of society.

Loneliness is social interaction without meaningful conversation, rather than being alone.

Moments of solitude are more precious than moments of pleasure.

SOCIETY/HUMOR

Humor

If you promise to be humorous, it never happens.

A belly laugh lives up to its origin.

House and Home

Home is a physical locus where our relaxed moments are programmed.

Most living rooms represent ennui rather than life.

If Americans used bidets, a culture might emerge.

Housewives require unusual management skills.

Chores bring satisfaction, but the results are seldom noticed.

The number of errands is directly proportional to the time available for errands.

Cleaning up for the cleaning woman requires more time than the cleaning woman devotes to cleaning.

To be productive at home, hire a quiet cleaning lady.

The only thing worse than household help is not having it.

HOUSE AND HOME

If your house were a castle, service people would still arrive without notice.

I wish I had a dime for every drink I have mixed for guests.

Dog owners resemble their dogs and lawyers their clients.

The distance between houses should exceed the range of a dog's bark.

Selling your house is physically draining and psychologically debilitating.

Neighborhood should be paramount in selecting a home.

Gardening creates a euphoria only excelled by napping.

Never return to your roots. Pain transcends memories.

Leisure Time

The more trained the mind, the more complex the leisure.

Diversions create more pleasure than expensive gifts.

My joys have seldom been related to anything I purchased.

A retreat narrows the gap between the Stone Age and the Space Age.

Rather than throwing bones in the corner of the cave, modern man sorts coins in his den.

The only thing wrong with birding is birders.

Art

If you want to feel old, review contemporary art.

Trash passes as art or a great deal of art is merely trash.

Affluence can perpetuate tasteless art.

Contemporary art repudiates intellect.

Interpretation of an artist's work does violence to creative intent.

Food

Leftovers can be tasty, but the entrée is a mystery.

The only problem with mixed nuts is the search for a cashew.

Happiness is chopsticks with chicken and walnuts and a fork with shrimp-fried rice.

Business breakfasts should be proscribed.

Only Boy Scouts and ranch hands should be forced to eat at tables for eight.

Sports

Baseball is a thinking man's sport. That explains the level of beer consumption at the ballpark.

When a national sport is played with the head rather than the hands, collective thinking may be muddled.

If you consider the Samboni a river in Africa, you are not a true hockey fan.

Are runners born strange, or does practice accentuate the trait?

If I could hunt duck hunters, I would not observe the limit.

LEISURE TIME/HOLIDAYS AND TRAVEL

Holidays and Travel

Travel sharpens our ability to make judgments about trivia.

In theory travel broadens. In practice it is merely painful.

We only travel if we can live the way we do at home.

Jet lag does not improve with practice.

The only thing worse than jet lag is never taking off.

Steerage and economy class are synonyms.

The country that produced the Pan-Am Clipper has become a second-rate aviation presence.

When I go to Hades, I will reserve a chariot rather than an automobile.

LEISURE TIME/HOLIDAYS AND TRAVEL

When you lock your keys in your car, you are convinced that your IQ approximates the temperature (Celsius).

Two weeks of auto travel with a friend is a trial by ordeal.

A vacation is a search for mediocrity which you cannot afford.

Taking annual leave to prepare a tax return is a perversion.

Health

Contemplating an operation pinpoints your vulnerability.

Calling a post-operative patient at the hospital is a belligerent act.

Donning your socks after an appendectomy is a real feat.

Convalescence is the therapy following confrontation with a hospital.

A quiet zone is a place far away from a hospital.

It is difficult to find a "caring" institution.

The most acute pain in dealing with the medical profession is the paper work.

HEALTH

Medical science may prolong life but not peace of mind.

Socialized medicine is wasteful and mediocre. Private enterprise medicine is exemplary and unfair.

The Three R's
Et Al

Thinking

People would rather talk than think.

My thoughts are more positive than my verbal expression.

Lone thought is only splendid when it is shared.

Whenever you are called a thinker, take cover.

Genius depends upon variable standards.

In the absence of envy, genius can flourish.

Originality begets enemies.

New ideas are not supported until they are old.

If an idea cannot be subjugated, we ignore it.

If we do not demand credit for an idea, progress is possible.

A moment of contemplation may be more meaningful than a lifetime of public posturing.

THE THREE R'S / THINKING

If all conversations were collected, they would be inundated by a single reflective moment.

If I could only remember the things I vowed to remember.

A bit of irrationality provides a stabilizing influence.

When the negative is isolated, the positive can emerge.

In contemporary America, thinking citizens are in hiding.

Sustained exposure can restrict informed opinion.

Accurate predictions are ignored. Inaccurate predictions become conventional wisdom.

It is better to prognosticate erroneously, than to be correct about a future we hope to avoid.

To be a social animal, spend some time in your den.

Reading

We are what we read as well as what we eat.

Life ebbs when reading becomes a chore.

Those who read seldom prattle.

A good book at bedtime is more critical than sleep.

A personal book collection reveals the story of a lifetime.

At age sixty-three, book acquisitiveness is replaced by liquidation.

Libraries tend to ignore reading requirements.

Biography: "The Way It Was According to Me."

THE THREE R'S / WRITING

Writing

Writing requires deeper thought than thinking.

Successful writing is characterized by trial and error, not virginal birth.

Good writing does not concentrate on the trivia of daily existence.

Without conflict, little of merit is written.

The written word is not necessarily superior. Christ wrote only once (with his finger in the dust).

When you write about "nameless characters," it is fortunate that they do not read.

Successful authors do not attempt to compose in public libraries.

Because they require privacy, writers are suspect.

Where you publish may be more important than what you write.

THE THREE R'S/WRITING

There is so much "cute" writing that the published word appears ugly.

Since satire attracts the mind and does not play upon emotion, it is disregarded in fiction.

I refuse to believe that what I have written has been written before.

Speaking

Words are spoken before meaning is understood.

He speaks more readily than he thinks.

He speaks more than his attainments warrant.

The American proclivity to talk, just talk, is boundless.

Good listeners are ignored.

People appear to listen as an excuse to continue talking.

If it is worth saying, it can be said quietly.

It is better to talk and say nothing than to remain silent and be considered anti-social.

Silence is only golden when ideas are more precious than gold.

Confidentiality is a trait lost in antiquity.

THE THREE R'S / SPEAKING

Until conversation begins, people are interesting.

In conversation, only the other guy is allowed to talk.

The wealthier the conversationalist, the more inane the conversation.

A dialogue requires two consenting adults who are interested in each other. Dialogues seldom occur.

Saying something nice without trying to be diplomatic is diplomacy.

Communication is endless, but it rarely begins.

When friends speak, that is gospel. When enemies speak, that is rhetoric.

A speaker's appearance is more important than content.

With sit-coms and sound bites, public speaking is obsolete.

When speaking, never correct an error.

Words

It is more important to choose words rather than friends wisely.

The distinction between profundity and obfuscation is profoundly obfuscated.

If a word eludes you, run for the dictionary rather than cover.

Certitude is inversely proportional to the number of words in your vocabulary.

Articulateness is considered glib.

Drivel is considered a universal language.

For every aphorism, somebody said it better.

If you feel a generalization coming up, swallow a specific.

The danger of generalizations is that major exceptions are controlling.

THE THREE R'S / WORDS

Wax, wane, ebb and flow—which way do the moon and tides go?

Sesame Street:

> Battle, brittle, bottle, Brest,
>   Man's rejoinder to life's bequest;
> Cattle, cuddle, coddle, chest,
>   Trivia united at Pavlov's behest.

The Venereal Game (with thanks to James Lipton):

- A bedlam of babies
- A bordello of Basset Hounds
- A tintinnabulation of tourists

Evolution of Words:

Old	New
"One Worlder"—Liberal	Globalist—Conservative
Democrat	democrat
Socialist	Liberal
Liberal	Communist
Communist	Deceased
Capitalist	God
Public Servant	Crook
"Red Neck"	Fundamentalist
Zealot	Republican
Educator	Entrepreneur
Athlete	Businessman

THE THREE R'S / WORDS

Acronyms:

ACNE   Association of Colleges of New England
ASS   (A Stuttgart German cooperative)
IRE   Institute of Radio Engineers
ASOL   (Does it really matter?)

"I" before "e" except after "c" (unless you are a deity).

He was an urbane rural expert.

A Lexicon of Verbs:

    Think — constantly   Work — religiously
    Speak — carefully   Eat — sparingly
    Read — voraciously   Relax — frequently
    Love — subjectively   Improve — remarkably
    Like — discriminatingly   Exercise — regularly
    Believe — reluctantly   Hope — longingly
    Admire — selectively   Live — gratefully
    Dislike — begrudgingly

The Media

Without a messenger, the message is useless.

Public perception is determined by selective truth.

Selective truth is too selective.

Without qualifying, the media allows you to enjoy sports and obituaries.

Freedom of the press does not insure an educated citizenry.

Today's news is not tomorrow's tee shirt, but it should be.

When television extols the virtues of a taxi driver, it is unlikely that the news will be substantive.

We spend more time selecting a television channel than a mate.

The television audience responds to the commentator, not to the comments.

THE THREE R'S / THE MEDIA

If I enjoyed television commercials, a "high five" might be appropriate.

The decibel level of canned television laughter is inversely proportional to the quality of programming.

A movie critic with sound judgment should change careers.

A fax transmits unimportant data too soon.

Except for sports, newspapers lack pathos.

If human beings were not venal or violent, we would not need the media.

Dreams

Dreaming is useful as long as you make allowance for chance.

A few who dream determine our destiny.

When my ship arrives, I will be waiting for baggage at the airport.

If dreaming were impossible, suicide would be inevitable.

Chance determines what we become. When we become it, it is difficult to become anything else.

DREAMS

Dreams:
Dreams verboten,
Dreams unleashed;
Dreams quixotic,
Creative sleep.

Dreams—Whose dreams?
Our dreams:
Remnants of decadent deities
Strangers to light.

Beliefs

"Out of sight, out of mind" (unless she is beautiful or he owes you money).

Relying upon inner strength is preferable to "letting it all hang out."

Charisma is more important than substance.

Form without substance produces form.

Context transcends content.

Time is a wasting asset which should not be dissipated.

We are reassured by the familiar and threatened by the unknown.

The unknown is more creditable than the known.

What webs we weave to disguise reality.

BELIEFS

Reality:
 Behold reality
  Respite illusive
 Miasmic tears
  Joys effete.

Virtue

Virtue is fictional.

With virtue, methodology is more important than practice.

Moderation is not perceived as a virtue.

Hope and despair originate with the same gene.

Unfulfilled hope is more palatable than hopelessness.

Profiles in courage do not always emanate from war or natural causes.

In a battle with integrity, "leverage" always wins.

Integrity and inevitability of change are the only sureties.

Honesty is the only virtue that is considered insincere.

VIRTUE

Rectitude is only right when it works.

Silence is a product of wisdom, not weakness.

When I speak, that is truth. When you disagree, that is prejudice.

If you are treated nicely, ignore the motive.

Respect for the time of others is the ultimate in courtesy.

Congeniality without manners is offensive.

Kindness breeds contempt.

"Thank you" and "excuse me" deserve redemption.

Sincerity is in shorter supply than common sense.

Heroes are increasingly transient.

Originality can only be copied, not taught.

Diverse interests may be perceived as weak character.

Vice

Without temptation, there is no vice or virtue.

We tend to endorse the temptations that tempt us.

If I wanted to live a life of sin, my financial status would intervene.

A sextet: three couples contemplating sin.

Sensitivity requires limited intelligence.

It is better to risk permanent alienation than a blow to the ego.

Miracles occur when ego flies.

Arrogance is sharing your greatness with others.

Personal limitations can be masked by hubris.

People with large egos have small stature.

When special favor is anticipated, principle is discounted.

VICE

We are touched by so much and affected by so little.

Taking offense slowly creates limited satisfaction.

Never forget a perceived slight.

There is no immunity from adversity.

We choose sides to dispute issues that cannot be resolved.

We tell lies to create a rationale for error.

If life is approached with a flair, you can fool everybody except yourself.

Envy does not nurture solicitude.

If he drowned and his body were missing, I would search upstream.

To commit a sin is human. To admit an error is a crime.

The Disciplines

History

History is a partial story told by a jingoist.

The nineteenth century represented warmth, color, time and slaves.

If I had lived in the nineteenth century, I would have been a serf rather than a cipher.

At historic sites, society dumps its garbage.

When judging the past, disregard contemporary standards.

Interpreting past deeds through current values is more sinful than re-writing history.

DISCIPLINES/HISTORY

History is created when the players amend the story.

If Jefferson had not purchased Louisiana, we would pay homage to the Black Madonna or the Union Jack rather than Thanksgiving.

Education

Illiteracy provides a conduit for misinformation.

Ignorance may be bliss, but it is still frightening.

Since educators confront ideas, they must be rebels.

Let's refine the elements in elementary education.

Ebonics sounds like the plague and deserves the same treatment.

With conservation rather than prayer, the curriculum might improve.

Higher education is lower than might be expected.

If college freshmen started as professors rather than students, they might be prepared for classes.

Professors will solicit funds for any purpose except teaching freshmen.

DISCIPLINES/EDUCATION

When faculties choose either labor or management, there will be time for teaching.

If the faculty ran the university, the same issues would be unresolved.

University presidents are preoccupied with marginal constituencies.

College officials distrust trustees and are glum about alums.

If you assume that the other guy is smarter, you are usually correct.

A society that pays athletes more than teachers runs stupidly.

Discrimination

All men are created unequal and spend their lives trying to catch up.

It is difficult to ignore your heritage.

Rudeness does not create equality.

If you want to discriminate, a rationale can be devised.

If we concentrate on discrimination, we fail to discriminate.

If you do not discriminate, your life is shallow.

Prejudice is practiced at a distance.

Sexual preference rules preclude normal social interaction.

When surnames do not produce snickers, anti-Semitism will disappear.

DISCRIMINATION

The most lethal discrimination is reserved for foreigners.

Courage is deleting "affirmative action" from an employment ad.

Even a melting pot leaves a residue.

The credo of the minority is generally correct (except when I am in the majority).

DISCRIMINATION / BLACKS

Blacks

Racial interaction presents a playing field for prejudice.

A prototype for discrimination—a male, urban, non-athletic Black teenager.

Relating to a person of color requires a smile.

Whites will endorse equal opportunity until Blacks are competitive.

Until Whites are comfortable with "Black Studies," full equality will be an illusion.

Disliking a neighbor should be provoked by action, not color of skin.

When Blacks are in the majority, they act like Whites.

Women

For gender equality, women must wear trousers or men must wear skirts.

Men are more willing for women to exercise leadership than women are willing to lead.

If women would select their advocates carefully, equality would prevail.

Women must only prove equality to themselves.

Work and Compensation

The Work Ethic

Man's reach should exceed his grasp but not by far.

Working is not the most enjoyable way to make a living.

When you work alone, there is no excuse for failure.

Natural talent with commitment leads to competence.

Success is cumulative because competence is assumed.

Incompetence over time is mistaken for commitment.

Experience tempers the optimist.

If you have not done it, it will be assumed that you cannot do it.

Progress is dependent upon compromise.

WORK/THE WORK ETHIC

We have difficulty agreeing on a compromise.

Promoting mediocrity facilitates mediocrity.

Work is being replaced by worker protection.

The amount of paper generated determines office satisfaction.

We opt for enjoyment rather than security and for security rather than a challenge.

Motivation:
   Touched by the crowd,
     Attracted to many;
   Affected by some,
     Motivated by a few.

Organization and Management

Policy makers excel in every field except policy.

When executives fail, policy makers intervene. When policy makers intervene, executives fail.

Failure is dependent upon the judgment of a superior rather than the weakness of a subordinate.

When you are fired, there is sympathy. When you resign, you are ignored.

For professional success, mentors are a prerequisite.

Competence is proven "on the job" and not through prior experience.

The only thing worse than dealing with a bureaucracy is working alone.

WORK/ORGANIZATION AND MANAGEMENT

The bureaucracy is amazed that action occurs without the intervention of the bureaucracy.

A planner repeats the conventional wisdom at the opportune moment.

When the results are clear, planners are recognized. Economists and management consultants are notorious exceptions.

Condemning the performance of others is easier than performing.

Except for business, the rewards for effective management are intangible.

Managers believe that the trappings of office inure to the person rather than the office.

Management reputations are built on a flair for public relations, a favorable economy, and a generous dose of luck.

A former chief executive officer is vestigial and should be excised from the corporate body.

Protecting an institution demands unique courage.

Business

Economics is more an art than a science.

Business is devoted to promoting profit rather than private enterprise.

Indecent profit cannot be made decently.

In small enterprise, social development and the profit motive are compatible.

Capitalism is on a roll, but the inequities are frightening.

Business can make money, but reform is an anathema.

Business and public policy are polar concepts.

Business abuses will be supplanted by the abuses of socialism.

Business news is duller than business.

WORK/BUSINESS

The will of the people is becoming the will of the entrepreneur.

Private enterprise does not champion the public interest unless the public intervenes.

The sanctions of private conscience can no longer control endemic corporate abuse.

Democracy and a global free market cannot coexist without free market restraints.

Customer service is a figment of imagination.

Privatization is replacing all other gospels.

Privatization provides the haves with more.

Business success is spawned by the misfortune of others.

Capitalism is ruining cultural values, but socialism failed to provide basic necessities for the masses.

Money

Money is not everything, but it comes close.

People with time and money can waste both.

If stockbrokers and fundraisers were not poor, playing with money would be fun.

Inheritance is the ethical way to become rich through investments.

Wealth pacifies private whims.

When you are poor, the wealthy appear smart.

Wealth may not be the answer, but it eliminates many questions.

The only thing worse than being poor is the promise of wealth.

Them that has keeps.

WORK / MONEY

Unless they have nothing, people do not live up to their surroundings.

It would be nice to be affluent, but the human costs are unacceptable.

We seldom possess the money we reputedly have.

Unless the gift is expensive, the thought is more important.

Wealth and taste do not correlate.

Tasteless affluence: Christie's auctioning a Louis XV lacquer commode.

A meaningful life depends upon taste; an enjoyable life upon money, and a cherished life upon both.

Adequate funds and a sense of timing insure progress.

Charity

Unless the gift is cash, charity is suspect.

Charitable gifts enhance the résumé and provide a tax deduction.

Patrons of the performing arts are seldom interested in the performance.

Charity is preoccupied with the plight of those who have been subjected to "acts of God."

Europeans recognize the artist rather than the donor.

The Public Weal

Democracy

Democracy is free will coupled with intelligent restraint.

In spite of facial warts, democracy has a winning smile.

Democracy relies upon collective rather than individual whim.

Freedom and individualism are not synonyms.

The distinction between individualism and selfishness is illusory.

For democracy to succeed, individualism must be subordinated.

Endorsing God and the flag cannot replace the thought process.

Democracy can only succeed if public responsibilities remain public.

PUBLIC WEAL / DEMOCRACY

Special interests must be curbed by public intervention.

Special interest groups trumpet refined opinions about nothing.

The essence of sound democracy: Government must be respected. Public service must be admired. Improved education must be financed with tax dollars. Responsibilities as well as rights must be stressed. Business must be a means rather than an end. Next week, we will discuss the tooth fairy.

It is difficult to be a patriot when your country tolerates the NRA.

The most desirable sentence of the court is house arrest.

I am proud of our nation's accomplishments. When I consider its potential, I cry.

PUBLIC WEAL/
GOVERNMENT

Government

If public officials do not exercise minimal control, commercial interests destroy the environment.

Public officials should be required to take public speaking.

Presidential transition studies suggest that the guy who held the job was incompetent.

The British shadow cabinet nurtures talent. The Presidential system wastes it.

Public service should not be suspect, and hope should not be out of season.

Government leaders are seldom trained for government service.

Politics

Political science is the study of mathematical probabilities devoid of a factual base.

Gimmickry and quackery stem from the same root.

There are two fields where talent is irrelevant: politics and punk rock.

With one-issue politics, political credos disappear.

Politicians have clear eyes because reading causes eyestrain.

Politics requires verbal facility and disdain for substance.

A pleonasm: "A controversial political appointee."

The politician who should be elected is not the politician who will be elected.

Liberals support revolution and abhor change.

PUBLIC WEAL / POLITICS

The only remaining tenet of the Liberal credo is being "green."

Mature adults are amalgams of liberal and conservative values or they run for office.

I like conservatives but deprecate their credo. I dislike liberals but endorse their message.

Left is right and right is wrong.

I would rather be wrong than a Republican and wealthy than a Democrat.

Voter illiteracy is preferable to electing bigots.

Virtually all politicians are consumed with polls rather than progress.

The presidential pulpit is banal, not bully.

The World Outside

Foreign Relations

Morality and foreign policy seldom meet.

Knowledge of foreign affairs is confined to the choice of vodka.

If an Ambassador shuns controversy, he or she will be promoted.

The cold war experts planned for every contingency except victory.

Converting a generation of brutal policemen into paragons of democratic virtue requires more than private enterprise.

In referring to Australia as "down under," there must be a redundancy.

Peaceful Orientals are as bellicose as Occidentals.

National characteristics may not be real, but they determine our reactions to every country.

WORLD OUTSIDE/FOREIGN RELATIONS

When you are distraught about a foreign culture, consider your own.

American tourists are obsessed with money, incessant chatter and deplorable dress.

Living abroad for a year may be more edifying than a decade at home.

When you return from overseas, you're treated like a defector.

Foreigners are impressed by the space, the pace, the scenery, and a Big Mac.

WORLD OUTSIDE / INTERNATIONAL AFFAIRS

International Affairs

Every human needs a homeland.

The ideal culture represents a merger of style and values from many nations.

Independence precedes interdependence.

In socialism, the trappings of privilege are disguised to suggest equality.

Modern communists are hungry, not doctrinaire.

If world leaders visited battlefields, there would be fewer wars.

Peace:
  Peace in my time,
    A drain on credulity;
  Man's inhumanity to man,
    The banal in perpetuity.

WORLD OUTSIDE / THE DEVELOPING WORLD

The Developing World

Before democracy can be exported, it must be packaged.

Democracy must be absorbed, not implanted.

US economic preoccupation is perceived as imperialism, not democracy.

We export munitions and pollution, but condemn the results.

People with money are not interested in Africa. People interested in Africa do not have money.

The British left solid institutions and bad feelings. The Portuguese left.

The developing world altered economies but retained despots.

When American Blacks are assigned to Africa, culture replaces color.

WORLD OUTSIDE / THE DEVELOPING WORLD

The developed world is not responding to the challenge of Africa, but neither is Africa.

Peace Corps impact is only perceptible to those who were part of it.

Unreliability, laziness and corruption were not spawned in the developing world.

About the Author

GLENN FERGUSON WAS US AMBASSADOR TO KENYA FROM 1966–69, for which he received the Arthur Flemming Award for outstanding government service. He has served as President of Radio Free Europe–Radio Liberty, Lincoln Center for the Performing Arts, Equity for Africa and four universities. He was the first Peace Corps Director in Thailand. In Washington, D.C., he was Peace Corps Associate Director and the first Director of VISTA. During the Korean War, he served as a US Air Force Officer. His second book, *Americana Against the Grain,* a collection of essays, will appear in the summer of '99. With his wife, Patti, he lives in Santa Fe, New Mexico.